The Nature Kid's Guide to
LIONS

RENATA MARIE

LP Media Inc. Publishing
Text copyright © 2023 by LP Media Inc.
All rights reserved.

For information address LP Media Inc. Publishing,
3178 253rd Ave. NW, Isanti, MN 55040
www.lpmedia.org

Publication Data

Lions
The Nature Kid's Guide to Lions — First edition.

Summary: "Learn all about Lions, the Nature Kid Way"
— Provided by publisher.

ISBN: 978-1-954288-62-1

[1. Lions – Non-Fiction] I. Title.

Title: The Nature Kid's Guide to Lions

CONTENTS

ON THE HUNT

Tall grass moves in Africa. Two big yellow eyes watch a zebra. A lion is on the hunt.

Lions live where they can easily hide from **prey**. They creep behind trees. They slide between bushes. **They wait in tall grasses.** Then—they strike!

FUN FACT!

Not all lions live in Africa. Asiatic lions live in India.

LARGE AND STRONG

Strong legs stay low. A long body creeps. Large, soft paws move quietly. A lion is ready to charge.

Lions hunt large animals. **They need size and strength to take them down.**

Lions can be four feet (1.2 meters) tall. Male lions weigh up to 550 pounds (249 kilograms). Female lions are called lionesses. They are smaller than male lions. They weigh up to 395 pounds (179 kg).

6 FEET

4 FEET

NIGHTTIME SNACK

The moon shines on hungry eyes.

Lions often hunt at night. Animals cannot see them. **But lions can see in the dark.**

Their ears turn to listen for the munch of grass. They open their mouths. They can taste the smell. If they like the taste, they will hunt the animal.

DID YOU KNOW?

Lions have claws. They go into their paws like house cat claws. This helps lions stay quiet when they hunt.

CHARGE!

The lioness races after the zebra.

Lions can run 50 miles (80 kilometers) per hour. **But they cannot run for very long.** Lions have small hearts and lungs. They tire easily. Their prey is fast. They must get close. They must run as hard as they can. And they must catch them quickly.

FUN FACT!

Lions can jump up to 36 feet. That's the length of a school bus!

SHARP TEETH

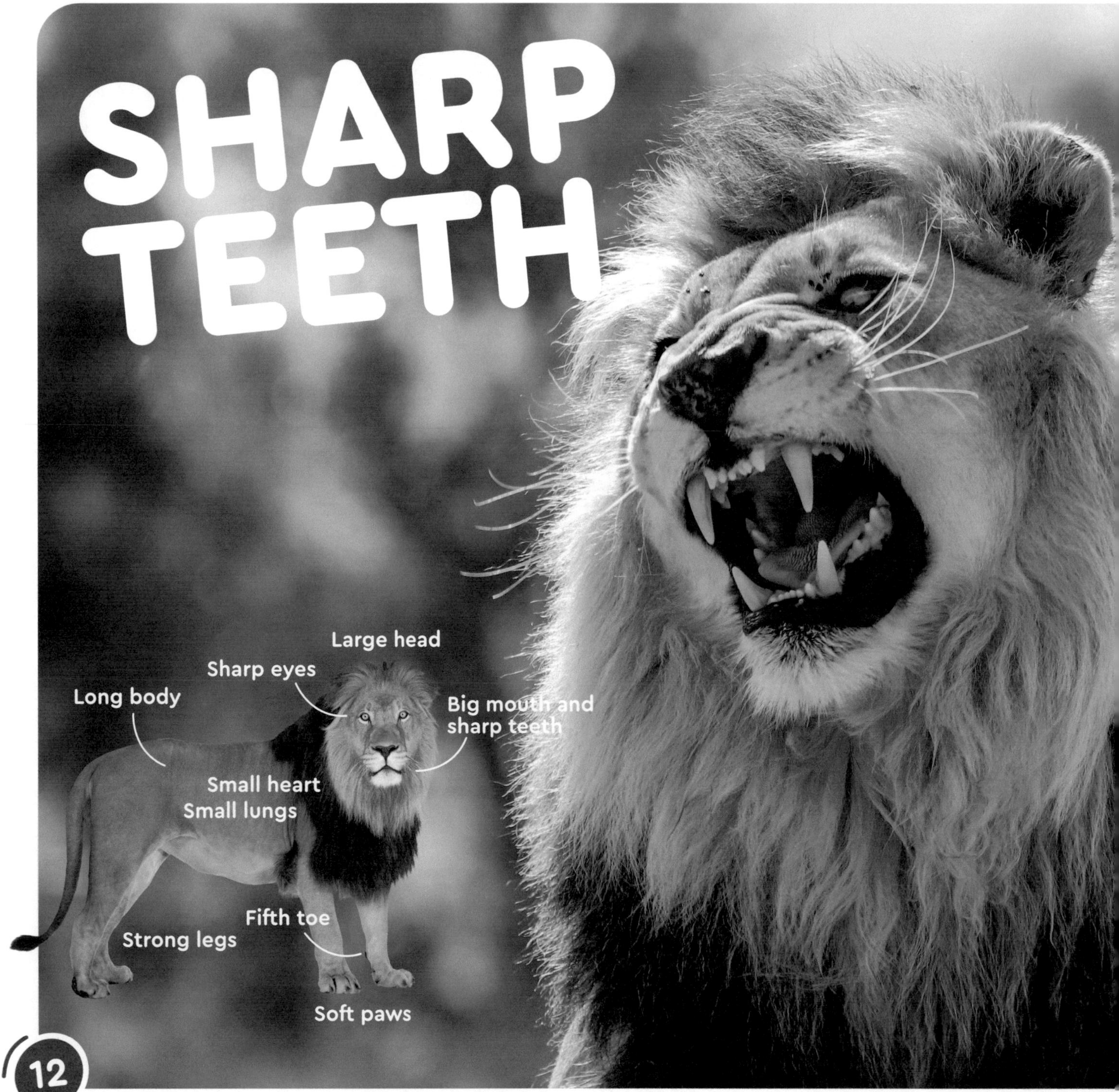

Large head

Sharp eyes

Long body

Big mouth and sharp teeth

Small heart
Small lungs

Fifth toe

Strong legs

Soft paws

Long, sharp teeth bite into a zebra.

Lions have large heads. And large mouths. **Their mouths are full of sharp teeth.** They use them to bite their prey. They hold their prey with their claws and bring the animal down.

When they eat, their teeth tear the meat. Lions have a fifth toe. They use it as a thumb to hold the meat down.

DID YOU KNOW?

Lions have one of the biggest bites on Earth. They can open their mouths 11 inches (28 centimeters) wide.

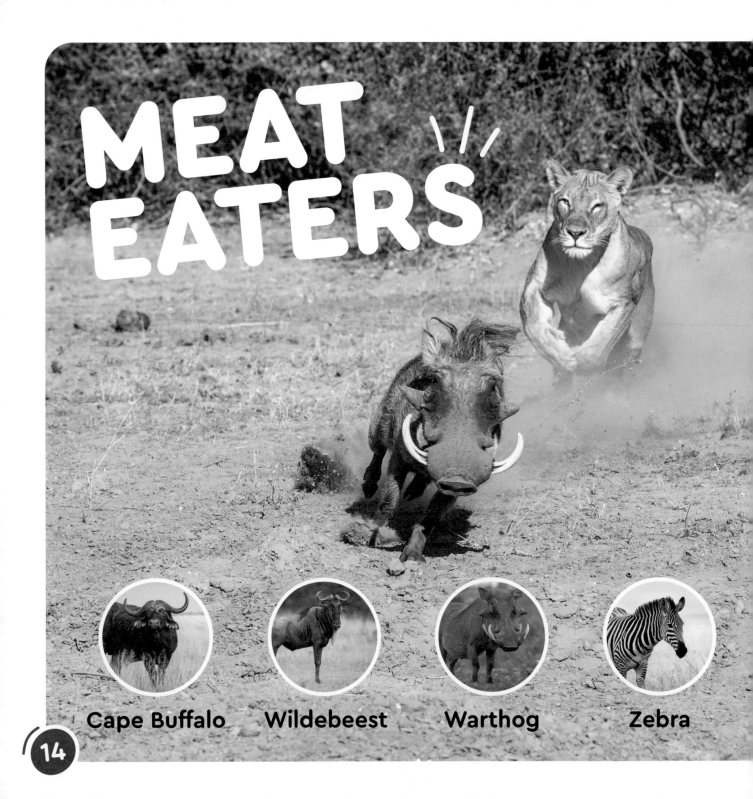

MEAT EATERS

Cape Buffalo   Wildebeest   Warthog   Zebra

The lioness licks her chops. Her kill is tasty.

Lions are carnivores. **They hunt almost everything.** They hunt zebras, antelopes, mice, warthogs, and hares. They hunt hippopotamuses, turtles, lizards, gazelles, birds, and crocodiles. They hunt wildebeests, giraffes, rhinoceros, Cape buffalos, and even young elephants.

Sometimes food is hard to find. Lions take the kills of leopards, cheetahs, and hyenas.

FUN FACT!

When water is hard to find, lions eat plants.

FAMILY PRIDE

A male lion keeps an eye on his pride.

Lions live in groups called prides. Each pride has one to three male lions. **The male lions keep the pride safe.** They mark their land to keep away other animals.

Males have large manes. The manes tell other lions to stay away. Manes also help lions show off for lionesses.

FUN FACT!

As lions grow older, their manes usually become darker.

ONE TEAM

FUN FACT!

Lions use the fluffy fur on their tails to talk to each other while hunting.

A storm darkens the land. The lionesses set out to hunt.

Male lions keep the young lions safe, and lionesses hunt. Their prey is often bigger and faster than them. **They have to work together to catch a meal.**

Lionesses usually hunt at night. They also hunt during storms. That way, their prey cannot see or hear them.

Lioness use teamwork. They creep closer to their prey. They circle it. Two charge. The prey tries to run, but it runs right into waiting claws.

HARD TO CATCH

A lioness bites a Cape buffalo, but it shakes her off.

Lions do not always catch their prey. **Groups only kill about one out of three animals they chase.** Lions that hunt alone catch even fewer animals.

And they have big stomachs. Males eat first. They can eat one-fourth of their body weight. Then the lionesses eat. Then the young lions.

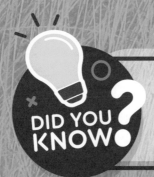

DID YOU KNOW? Lions only eat every three to four days.

CATNAP

The sun is hot. The lions are full. They take a nap.

After a night of hunting, lions are tired. They sleep—a lot. **Lions rest for 20 hours each day.**

The lions find shade. They climb trees to rest. They spend time with their pride. They rub heads and lick each other. They watch young lions play.

FUN FACT!

Lion tongues have hard bumps. They can remove meat from bones. They also use them to clean their fur.

LITTLE LIONS,

Leopard

Hyena

African Wild Dog

Meow. A little lion wakes up.

Lion babies are called cubs. They are born helpless. They are small. They do not open their eyes until they are a week old.

Lionesses give birth to their cubs in a safe place. They find a bush or a cave.

Adult lions do not have **predators**, but cubs do. Tigers, hyenas, leopards, and even other lions hunt cubs.

The mother will keep her cubs safe. The cubs will go back to the pride when they can keep up. This is usually when they are six weeks old.

FUN FACT!

Lions are born with spots or stripes on their fur.

MOTHERS
TOGETHER

A lioness licks a cub. She acts like the cub's mother, but she is her aunt.

Lionesses can have up to six cubs. All of the cubs in the pride grow up together.

Lionesses in a pride are often sisters. They all feed the cubs milk. They all watch out for hungry predators. They keep the cubs away from big elephants and buffaloes.

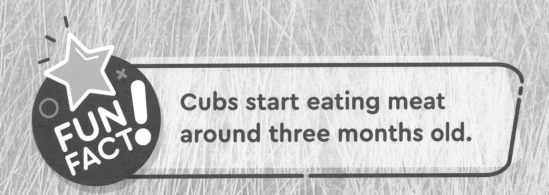

FUN FACT!

Cubs start eating meat around three months old.

PLAYFUL CATS

A cub jumps onto her sister's back. They roll through the grass.

Cubs charge. They chase. They bite. They are learning to hunt.

Lions become adults when they are two years old.

Lionesses usually stay with their pride. **But males are kicked out.** They often stay in a group with their brothers, or they find other male lions. Then they look for a new pride to take over.

DID YOU KNOW?

Lionesses use the fluff on their tails to tell their cubs to follow them.

ROCKING ROAR

Roars rock the land.
A pride is showing its power.

Lions roar together. Even young cubs will meow. **Lions have the loudest roar of big cats.**

Lions roar to find each other. They roar to tell other animals to stay away. Their roars can be heard from five miles (8 km) away.

Lions make other sounds too. They growl, hiss, snarl, puff, and grunt.

FUN FACT!

Prides can have three to 40 lions.

FALLEN KINGS

Lions were once the kings of Africa.

They lived all over Africa. They lived in Asia. They even lived in Europe. Now they live on small pieces of land. Most of the land is broken up across Africa. There are only 20,000 lions left in the wild.

Lions are **vulnerable** animals. **What happened to all of the lions?**

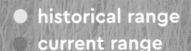

● historical range
● current range

NO PREY

A lioness tries to cross a road. She hopes to find food.

Humans moved across Africa. They built towns and roads. They built farms. They pushed the animals out.

Lions could not get to other lions. Pride sizes became smaller.

Less land means fewer animals to hunt. And the Earth is warming. The hotter it becomes, the less grass there is. And that means fewer animals for lions to eat.

KIDS CAN HELP THE EARTH

Plant a tree

Grow your own vegetables and fruits

Turn the lights off

HUNTING THE HUNTER

A lioness creeps toward a farm. She is hungry. And the sheep look tasty.

When there is less prey, lions hunt farm animals. Farmers try to keep themselves and their animals safe. They shoot at the lions.

Other people kill lions too. They want to sell their teeth, bones, claws, and skin. Some people hunt them for fun.

DID YOU KNOW?

Lion teeth can be four inches (10 cm) long.

SLEEPING SAFELY

A lion sleeps peacefully in a park.

People are trying to help lions. They built parks. They took traps out of the wild. They built walls around farm animals. They keep an eye out for illegal hunters.

People hope that one day, lions and humans can live safely side by side.

FUN FACT!

Lions also live in zoos. People take care of them. They keep them safe.

GLOSSARY

carnivores
animals that eat meat
page 15

lungs
the part of the body that
helps animals breathe
page 10

predators
animals that hunt
other animals
page 25

prey
animals that are hunted
by other animals
page 4

pride
a group of lions
page 16

vulnerable
in danger
page 33

MORE AMAZING ANIMAL BOOKS
from Nature Kids Publishing!

The Nature Kid's Guide to
GIRAFFES
Level 2

A LEVEL 2 READER FOR CURIOUS YOUNG **KIDS** WHO LOVE GIRAFFES!

RENATA MARIE

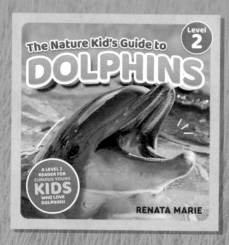

The Nature Kid's Guide to
DOLPHINS
Level 2

A LEVEL 2 READER FOR CURIOUS YOUNG **KIDS** WHO LOVE DOLPHINS!

RENATA MARIE

The Nature Kid's Guide to
RABBITS
Level 2

A LEVEL 2 READER FOR CURIOUS YOUNG **KIDS** WHO LOVE RABBITS!

RENATA MARIE

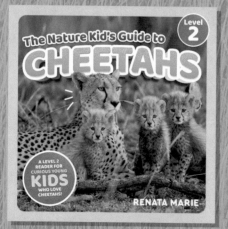

The Nature Kid's Guide to
CHEETAHS
Level 2

A LEVEL 2 READER FOR CURIOUS YOUNG **KIDS** WHO LOVE CHEETAHS!

RENATA MARIE

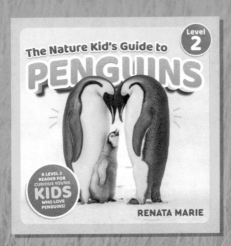

The Nature Kid's Guide to
PENGUINS
Level 2
A LEVEL 2 READER FOR CURIOUS YOUNG KIDS WHO LOVE PENGUINS!
RENATA MARIE

The Nature Kid's Guide to
PANDAS
Level 2
A LEVEL 2 READER FOR CURIOUS YOUNG KIDS WHO LOVE PANDA BEARS!
RENATA MARIE

The Nature Kid's Guide to
OWLS
Level 2
A LEVEL 2 READER FOR CURIOUS YOUNG KIDS WHO LOVE OWLS!
RENATA MARIE

The Nature Kid's Guide to
MEERKATS
Level 2
A LEVEL 2 READER FOR CURIOUS YOUNG KIDS WHO LOVE MEERKATS!
RENATA MARIE

Visit NatureKidsPublishing.com
to Learn More!

Made in the USA
Columbia, SC
24 March 2024

33536177R00024